With Bee... ...s

HALIFAX

HALIFAX

Photographs by Sherman Hines

Halifax
NIMBUS PUBLISHING LIMITED
1988

HALIFAX

Copyright Nimbus Publishing Limited, 1988
ISBN 0-920852-12-2
Third Printing – September 1985
Fourth Printing – September 1986
Fifth Printing – September 1988
Sixth Printing – September 1990

Nimbus Publishing Limited
P.O. Box 9301
Station A
Halifax
Nova Scotia
Canada
B3K 5N5

To my sister Lorraine

Most photographs taken with Pentax 6 x 7; others with Nikon 35mm.

Thanks to Maritime Colour Lab for all processing of Ektachrome film.

Printed in Hong Kong by
The Everbest Printing Company Limited

Foreword

Halifax has been my home, my place of business and my environmental studio since 1965.

After graduating from photography school in California in 1968, I made the decision to return to Halifax to continue my part-time business of photography. The city of Halifax (and Nova Scotia) still seemed to have a special place in my life even after travelling most of North America, Mexico and Europe.

With my special interest in historic architecture, Halifax always seemed to me a treasure chest of discovery. It was during one of my many photographic trips around the city that I discovered the West House. Ten years later I had the pleasure of restoring it to a useful life once again.

Halifax, with its parks and gardens has been a great inspiration to me as a professional photographer, for it has provided the setting for many family and children's portraits over the years. I have come to know every swan, tree, rock and nook over the years and have enjoyed every minute of it.

When I began to photograph for this book, it was difficult not to make a very narrow personal statement with my photographs, so I worked harder to produce a broader, more diversified image of the city I have loved for the past sixteen years. We tend to make judgements about the places where we live coloured by the experiences and friendships that we find in each. I hope that you will feel some of the joy and affection I have for this city of Halifax and that these images will give you a lasting and exciting portrait of a Canadian city which has been an important part of my life.

Sherman Hines.

Introduction

"Halifax? Grey, cold, wet, and dirty. You can't imagine how bloody awful the place was during the War." Such was the conventional wisdom in Upper Canada when I moved down to Halifax in 1970. Driving in from the western approaches, there were a few intriguing glimpses of the place, but Vancouver, Capetown, or Rio it wasn't. Nor was it Montreal, Toronto, or Calgary, for that matter.

So what was it? Understated, for one thing. There were elegant buildings, but no grand ones. There were charming, comfortable streets, but no spectacular boulevards. Halifax was, in short, everything a sensible eighteenth century European provincial garrison town should be. Founded in 1749, dominated by the Citadel, the harbour, and the military, Halifax's original streets were laid down in the familiar grid pattern of the European walking city. Through a crucial accident of geography, this humane and civilized scale of living has been preserved into the late twentieth century. The development of Halifax was forcibly and fortunately constrained by the absolute physical limitation of being virtually surrounded by the sea.

Halifax's only Canadian rival is Quebec, and these two old cities have more in common than their history, their heritage buildings, and their European sense of place. They are, respectively, the true cultural capitals of English and French Canada. Halifax is the purest expression of the best historic traditions of English Canada. Still Loyalist, ceremonial, church-going and conservative, Haligonians are also relaxed, self-assured, well-informed, and ironic. The town is not long on ostentation or stylishness, but its inhabitants are genuinely warm-hearted, fun-loving and hospitable (even to interlopers from Upper Canada!).

In the last decade, Halifax has changed dramatically, and for the better. While preserving its traditions, institutions, and a significant number of its streetscapes, the place has exploded with new people, businesses, restaurants, and cultural amenities. For all its conservatism, Halifax is an open, tolerant, civilized city in which a great variety of people, interests, and tastes seem to jostle quite happily together. Indeed, on some summer days, the place seems quite Mediterranean.

Those of us who have been converted to the city believe we have stumbled upon one of Canada's best kept secrets. Now that we are here, we feel the drawbridge should be raised. But alas, the secret is getting out, and I am afraid this book by my friend Sherman Hines will do nothing to discourage the thundering hordes. But before you get any funny ideas about moving down, let me tell you how dreadful the place was during the War . . . . .

Dr. John F. Godfrey
President & Vice Chancellor
University of King's College

The city is pleasantly situated on the eastern slope of a peninsula formed by Chebucto Harbor and a branch of the sea known as the North West Arm . . . Chebucto Bay, terminating in the Harbor, contracting at the "Narrows", and again widening out into Bedford Basin, is, taken altogether, one of the great havens, not of this continent only, but of the world, whether for beauty, safety, or capaciousness, having few equals, and, so far as Canadians believe, no superior. Along the water front of the peninsula alluded to, for about three miles the streets and houses of the city rise tier upon tier, until the summit of the slope is crowned by the Citadel, a massive fortification two hundred and fifty feet above tide water, and bristling with huge guns of the latest construction, — emblems significant indeed are these latter, of Imperial power and connection, but except blank powder, they and those of the fortresses in the vicinity of Halifax, have as yet slept idly in their embrasures. But to return; whether seen from the eastern or western passages of the harbor, or from the islands at its mouth, which break the rude force of the Atlantic or still better, when viewed from the town of Dartmouth, Halifax is a city fair to behold.

from *The Halifax Guide Book*, C.C. Morton, Halifax 1878, courtesy of Public Archives of Nova Scotia.

From the *London Magazine*, 1760.
Courtesy of the Nova Scotia Legislative Library.

List of Plates

1. On the edge of Citadel Hill overlooking the city is the Town Clock. It was commissioned by Edward, Duke of Kent, (father of Queen Victoria) during his stay in Halifax as military commander (1749-1800). His passion for punctuality and mechanical devices prompted him to have the clock placed in a prominent position above the city.

2. Stretching across the narrows from the north end of the peninsula the Murray MacKay Bridge links the twin cities of Halifax and Dartmouth.

3. George's Island, in the middle of Halifax Harbour, was formerly part of the inner defences of the harbour. The fortifications are now abandoned and the lighthouse stands alone.

4. Fishing boats bring their daily catch to Fisherman's Market in downtown Halifax.

5, 6. Not only the port, but also shipbuilding and repair, bring vessels from many parts of the world to Halifax. This view shows the repair dock at the shipyards in Halifax.

7. With all that comes and goes in a busy harbour, the seagulls maintain their scavenging guardianship over all.

8. A boat returns from a winter's fishing trip with ice-coated rails and rigging. One of the dangers of a winter sea is that the weight of the ice on the ship can raise the centre of gravity and render the vessel top heavy. Seamen spend long hours chipping ice.

9. This view shows the Angus L. Macdonald Bridge leading from North Street in Halifax to Dartmouth. This is the older of the two bridges, and was erected in 1955.

10. The ferry service between Halifax and Dartmouth provides excellent transit service for commuters and shoppers.

11. This sturdy sailing craft bears the design and rig of a fishing boat from the days of sail.

12. Ships of the Canadian Navy are reminders that Halifax has been a strategic point in the North Atlantic since the British founded the city in 1749 as a base from which to conduct campaigns against the French.

13, 14, 15, 16. The container terminal in Halifax is now a prominent feature in the landscape. Goods transported around the world make the land and sea link at the southern tip of the peninsula. Facilities will soon be expanded with the addition of another terminal at the north end of the city.

17. Port activity includes the exporting of grain to third world countries. Container shipping has not eliminated the role of the stevedore elsewhere in the port.

18. The port is able to enjoy year-round business in spite of the harsh winters which ice up many other eastern Canadian ports.

19. Weather vain located on top of the World Trade and Convention Centre in downtown Halifax.

19a. The World Trade and Convention Centre, looking up Citadel Hill.

20. Historic Properties seaboard walkway, heavily populated with the summer lunch time crowds.

21. Looking south-east from Citadel Hill, the mouth of the harbour opens beyond George's Island.

22. This statue of Winston Churchill stands on the grounds of the city library. Its presence was made possible by a committee who collected private donations. The sculptor is Oscar Niemann.

23. In the heart of the city is the Grand Parade with St. Paul's Church on the south, City Hall on the north, and the financial district descending east to the waterfront.

24. Toronto Dominion Bank Tower on Barrington Street.

25. The Historic Properties reflected off the waters of Halifax Harbour.

26. Maritime Tel and Tel office tower at the lower end of Spring Garden Road.

27. The first of the downtown restoration projects was completed on the east side of Granville Street. This view shows the more recently completed west side, a fine example of Italianate architecture.

28, 29. Historic Properties is the name of the group of buildings on the waterfront that were restored and reconstructed and now house over thirty shops and a dozen restaurants. The stone building called the Privateer's Warehouse, includes a pub and two restaurants, a sail loft and the office for harbour tours aboard the schooner, BLUENOSE II.

30. The cenotaph in the Grand Parade.

31. On the north side of the Grand Parade, City Hall maintains its Victorian dignity against the backdrop of Scotia Square.

32, 33. St. Paul's Anglican Church (1750), which faces City Hall, is the city's oldest surviving building. In early years the Anglicans shared the building with Dissenters, Micmacs and German Protestants, each Sunday at an appointed time.

34. King's College, est. 1789, was the first college in Nova Scotia. Retaining its Anglican traditions it is now affiliated with Dalhousie University.

35. Dalhousie University was founded in 1818 by the ninth Earl of Dalhousie. It is one of the largest universities in Atlantic Canada and is renowned for its medical and law schools and gaining recognition in the new field of oceanography.

36. The Harrington House on Morris Street dating back to the 1820s, won a Heritage Canada Award in 1977 for restoration by the owners, Frank and Jean Harrington. The granite blocks used in this style of construction were sometimes transported from Scotland as ballast in the hulls of wooden ships.

37. The tree-shaded sidewalks of Young Avenue in the prosperous South End, close to Point Pleasant Park.

38. The Lutheran church on Brunswick Street was built by German settlers around 1750.

39. Shipbuilding skills and the availability of wood make wooden houses of this style a characteristic part of towns and cities on the Atlantic coast.

40. At the scene of a dramatic fire which destroyed the United Church on Brunswick Street.

41. Night time traffic on Tower Road.

42. In the nineteenth century, Brunswick Street was the fashionable district where wealthy merchants lived. Unfortunately time brought decay and the dilapidation of many of these architectural gems, but happily in recent years renewed interest in the preservation of historic buildings has brought new life to the area.

43. St. Patrick's Convent on Brunswick Street.

44, 45. West House, 2319 Brunswick Street, was built in 1867 and restored in 1976 for Sherman Hines' studio.

46. Winter comes every year and paints a new landscape in a white shroud.

47. From a vantage point along the North West Arm an early riser can catch the sun rising out of the sea.

48, 49, 50. Fleming Park, also called the Dingle, is the site of a large tower which was erected by the Canadian Clubs in commemoration of the advent of represent-ative government in Nova Scotia in 1758. The land was donated to the city by Sir Sandford Fleming, a Scottish philanthropist, and a former vice-president of Canadian Pacific Railroads.

51, 52. Yacht racing is a favorite pastime for many Haligonians.

53, 54. BLUENOSE II, the replica of the famous schooner BLUENOSE, was commissioned by the Oland family of Halifax and launched in 1963. With a full-time crew she sails to various corners of the world representing Nova Scotia and Canada as a symbol of goodwill and fine boatbuilding traditions. During summer months she sails daily tours around Halifax Harbour from her berth in Historic Properties.

55, 56, 57, 58. The star-shaped Citadel, on the hill overlooking the harbour around which the city has grown, was the central point of the defence system. Largely the work of the Duke of Kent in the latter part of the eighteenth century, it is now being restored by Parks Canada as a museum focussing on military history and artifacts.

59. Every September Halifax takes on the festive spirit in memory of the famous journalist and former premier of the province, Joseph Howe.

60. Natal Day, the founding of Halifax in 1749, is remembered each year in July. This parade through downtown streets is the beginning of the day of celebration.

61. Nova Scotian fare reflects the varied ethnic backgrounds of the residents. Halifax boasts a fine selection of restaurants to accommodate all tastes. (clockwise from top left) A roast goose is traditional for Christmas; lobster cooked, hot or cold is always a favorite; a lobster raw is less appetizing; fresh fruit and vegetables complement any meal.

62. In Privateer's Warehouse on the top deck, a master chef has prepared a lobster to look as good as it tastes.

63. (clockwise from top left) Point Pleasant Park on the southern tip of the peninsula offers many pastoral pleasures including birdwatching; in keeping with a Scottish heritage a bagpiper can be heard daily at the Lord Nelson Hotel; Halifax prides iteself with a town crier; keeping fit and healthy on a fine summer's day does not exclude time out for a chat.

64. Gerald O'Brian keeps a watchful eye on Argyle Street and can be persuaded to sell a book or two.

65. Outside the Public Gardens from the first day of Spring to the first day of winter, artists and craftsmen offer their work for sale.

66. Dutch Mason and his blues band, Nova Scotia's native sons, play regularly in Halifax nightclubs.

67. "Is there room in there for me?"

68. This charming bandstand in the Public Gardens, was donated to the city by Queen Victoria.

69, 70. The Public Gardens were laid out in the 1870s by Richard Power, who had been head gardener to the Duke of Devonshire in Ireland. It was Joseph Howe who instigated the founding of a horticultural society which developed the gardens. There are over one hundred varieties of trees and ninety varieties of plants. Species of ducks come south in the winter for a stay in the Public Gardens.

71, 72. Point Pleasant Park offers a hundred and one places to play for young and old. From the beach area to the forts and nature trails, there is an endless variety of landscapes in the 186 acres of park.

73, 74. The Prince of Wales Tower in Point Pleasant Park is one of the many historic landmarks in the park. It was built in 1796 as part of the defences for the harbour.

75. Winter sets in with a snowstorm. In this view of Citadel Hill many Haligonians are reminded of the tragic explosion on December 6, 1917 when a freighter and an ammunition ship collided in the harbour. The death toll was 1700, and countless were injured. The homeless collected on Citadel Hill only to be nearly frozen in a snowstorm the following day.

76, 77. Out in the harbour at night Christmas lights decorate the naval vessels.

78. Like a flock of birds on the water, these sailing boats are pointing to the mouth of the harbour, out to sea.

2

6

8

9

13

21

23

24

IN HONOUR OF
THOSE WHO SERVED

IN MEMORY OF
THOSE WHO FELL

1914   1918
1939   1945

33

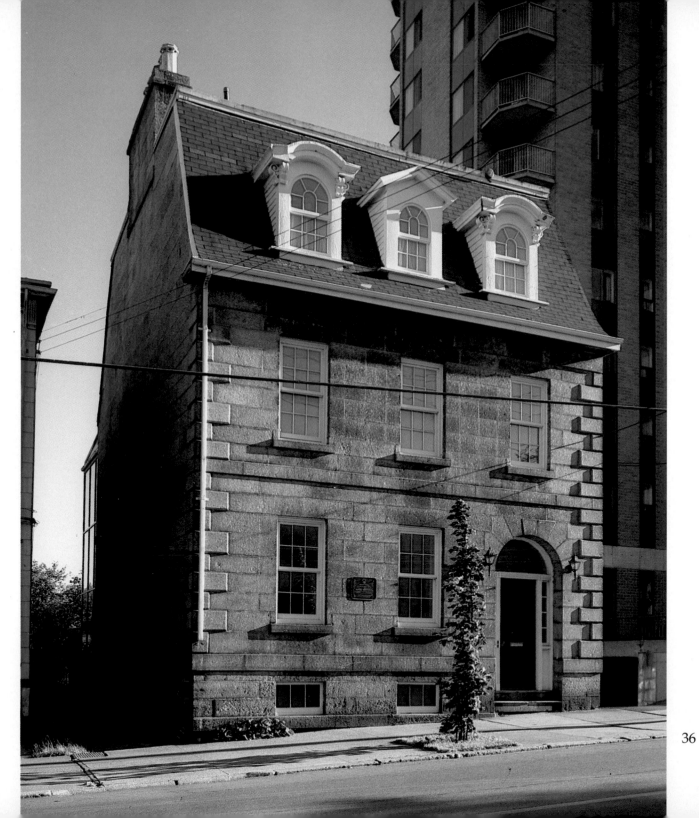

38

44

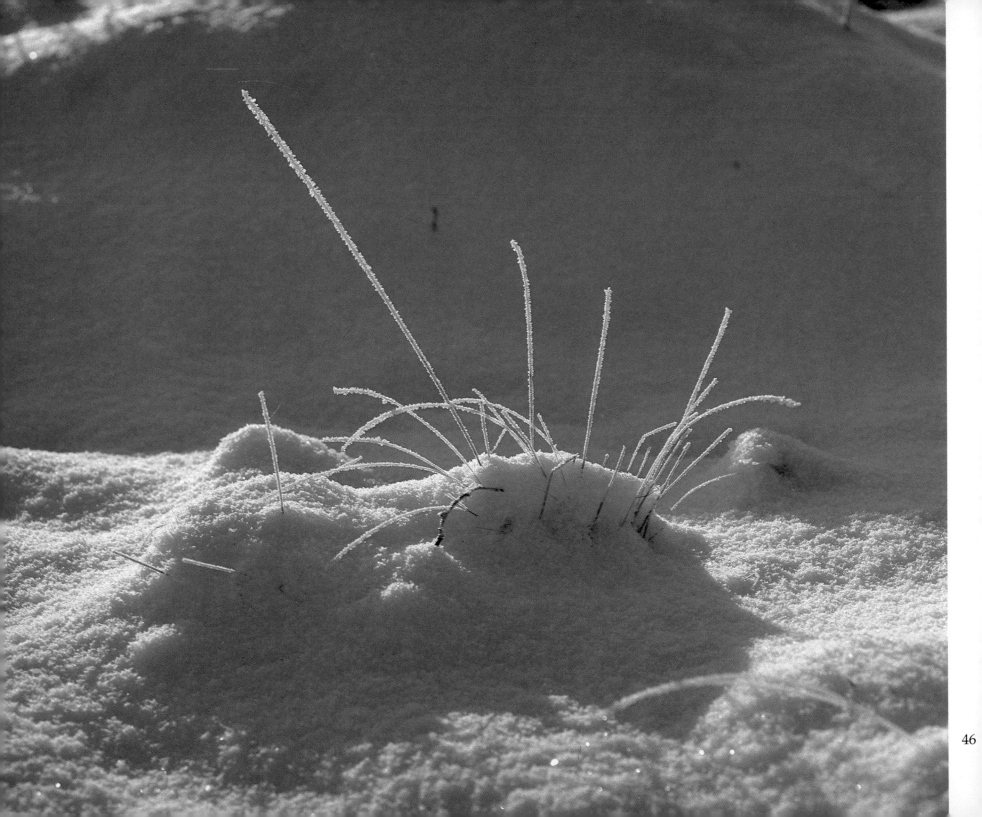

59

63

WAS $12.00
8"X16"
NOW $5.00 = ea.

½ PRICE
WAS $3.00
NOW $1.50

65